Zenyatta/Joanna

Two Poets: One Equine/One Human

poems by

Joan Dobbie

Finishing Line Press
Georgetown, Kentucky

Zenyatta/Joanna

Two Poets: One Equine/One Human

Copyright © 2023 by Joan Dobbie
ISBN 979-8-88838-166-3 First Edition
All rights reserved under International and Pan-American Copyright Conventions. No part of this book may be reproduced in any manner whatsoever without written permission from the publisher, except in the case of brief quotations embodied in critical articles and reviews.

ACKNOWLEDGMENTS

I would like to thank Eugene's KLCC (Lane Community College Radio) for introducing me to Zenyatta, and YouTube Inc. for pulling me into her life. The poem "There are Jockeys.." appeared in either *Verseweavers* or the *Oregon Poets Concord Anthology* some years back. Thank you to both the Oregon Poets Association (OPA), and Sandy Ellston of the Poets Concord for incredible conferences and community. And thank you to the Oregon poetry community altogether for welcoming me into its heart from the moment I appeared on the scene in 1983 to the present day. Thank you to Quinton Hallet for first mentioning Finishing Line Press to me, and to Claudia Lapp, for reading the manuscript and her gift of a "Girl Power" poster honoring Zenyatta. Special thanks to Erica Goss for writing a "blurb" for this book, and for planning her own April birthday celebration as a book release party for Zenyatta/Joanna. Special thanks to all the various organizations worldwide that take in equine retirees. And most special of all, thank you, Zenyatta, for enriching my life.

Publisher: Leah Huete de Maines
Editor: Christen Kincaid
Cover Design: Elizabeth Maines McCleavy
All poetry, artwork and photography by Joan Dobbie

Order online: www.finishinglinepress.com
also available on amazon.com

Author inquiries and mail orders:
Finishing Line Press
PO Box 1626
Georgetown, Kentucky 40324
USA

Table of Contents

November 5, 2010 1
My Team Z 2
Alchemy 3
Sweet Lisa Sings Me My Song 4
Why We run 6
The Auction 7
In the Silence of Speed 8
Flower Dream 9
Breeders Choice 2010… 10
My Good Name 11
There are jockeys 12
Ruffian 13
Zenyatta Retired 15
My Own Silver Stable 16
Because My Plane was Late 17
It's Sad to See the Horses out to Pasture 19
Nightmare 20
Lanes End Farm Teaser 21
Zenyatta's on top of the world 22
Trainer John Visits Lanes End 23
Sheik Muhammad bin Khalifa bin Saeed Al Maktoum 24
The Breeding Barn 25
To My Unborn Foal 26
Zenyatta No Longer "In foal" 27
These Are the Races I Won 28
Afterword 29
Postscript 30

Dear Zenyatta,

I write poems. That's what I do in life. I also teach yoga. And sometimes I make sculptures, or paintings or drawings. None of them are as beautiful as the bronze of you dancing I'm hoping to win with these words. I heard about you for the first time on Public Radio the day before the Breeders Cup 2010. I looked you up on YouTube. I fell in love. When you placed 2nd the next day, my heart broke & I loved you even more. So far I have written 17 poems in your honor. I'm hoping to write I don't know how many more or for how long I'll be writing them. I plan to put them together into a book which I'll illustrate myself, out of love and memory. Every day I find new videos of you on YouTube. If I'm sad, they make me happy. I love watching you fly past the others with Mike on your back. I love watching you win. I love watching you dance. I love watching you love your friend, John. I love watching you kiss pretty Lisa, while she's singing your song. I even love watching you prance with your new equine friends out there at Lane's End, tails waving like flags in the wind. Thank you for being, Zenyatta.

With love,
Joanna

November 5, 2010
by Joanna

Of course they have stars in Hollywood
but did you know they have horses?

There in her barn 55 lives Zenyatta
Queen of the Equines

Winner of Race after Race after Race
Beloved of women the wide world over

Zenyatta who starts at the end
& ends at the start again
     & again
        & again
          & again
She proves in our hearts
that we females are worthy

Again & Again & Again & Again

& tomorrow she races her final race
If tomorrow the winner

—as always the winner—

Proof she will be that the Goddess
Can take Equine form

My Team Z
by Zenyatta

There are every day of my life
at least 14 humans
who love me up close

& thousands of fans who love
at a distance
& I love them back, every one

Here at my Barn 55 are the Moss's
(my owners) who come by
with carrots & praises

Mario who grooms me
& grazes me
   & makes me feel clean,

John, my mentor, who teaches me goodness
—what is expected of me every day—

I am bathed, petted, praised & pampered
honored for the speed that is native to me
as my breath

& most precious is my Mike
who shares this with me on the track
to the cheers of the crowds

He says I'm the greatest he's ever ridden
If I am his vehicle, he is my Lord,
the invisible angel
perched on my back

driving me home

Alchemy
      by Zenyatta

I'm wanting to say how special it is
between me and my John, how much

we two love one another. Some nights
he sleeps in my stall & those nights
I am bathed in sweet dreams

John is my mentor, my teacher, the one being
I depend on the most. I truly believe that it's
John made me great

Before there was John in my life
I was feisty, wild, hard to handle. I'll bet
my nickname was "Trouble"

But John picked up my Power
like a handful of mud & with his gentle ways
he turned it to gold—Liquid Gold—

gold as that full bowl of Guiness
he gives me for *Thank you*
after yet another great race—

Sweet Lisa Sings Me My Song
by Zenyatta

One day I was outside my barn 55
grazing with my Mario

when this pretty blond human came over

to sing me my song she had written
all about my greatness

& there she stood singing
just for me

& there I stood munching my grass
that they grow just for me

& I couldn't help but look up
& walk over & give her a kiss

on the face & then I kept nuzzling
my soft horsey nose

closer & closer to her tiny human feet

(where she stood on my grass
made delicious by her feet)

& then she started to giggle
& step away

giggle & back out of my way though

she kept right on singing her song
about my greatness, though shyly

I think she was shy to be so very close
to ME in real life

I think that she thinks I'm a Goddess

my dear John, as ever,
at the camera

Why We Run
> *by Zenyatta*

We live to run. We fly over the track as
they watch & they cheer—$$$ signs buzzing
their eyes. In $$$ they measure our greatness.
In millions & billions of $$$. Our racing

is built upon $$$ for them. It's the $$$
that make their world good. But for us, it's the speed
that we live for—They create us for $$$—
but we run because running is our greatest need.

We run because running is all that there is
not to outrun one another for $$$.
No—that is *their* sickness—but simply for this:
to run & run faster
              & faster
                           & faster
Like those planets that circle a raging hot sun
Nothing can stop us. We are born to run

The Auction
by Joanna

As Zenyatta—the yearling—
(not yet Zenyatta) was bought

by David Ingordo, of course for the Moss's
(we all know
this in retrospect) for only $60,000
just like any other thoroughbred yearling
on the auction block

a bored looking black woman
was leading her forward & backward
showing off her good breeding,
her fine Arabian features,
downplaying the ringworm
that troubled her skin

& I couldn't help but think
of my country, America's, foul history
of blatant human slavery,
whose shadow still darkens
our every waking day
(though it hides in the shadows)

In due time my beloved Zenyatta
—now used as a brood mare—will give birth
to yet another slave

In the Silence of Speed
   by Zenyatta

In the days when we ran
they would plug up our ears
so that we couldn't hear

our hooves pounding
the ground
& we lived in the awesome
silence of speed—
in the nothing, no
             nothing, no
nothing but speed

in which we were brave
& the braver we were, the faster
we flew

like those gliders that slide through the sky
without engines

we flew through the heavenly
silence of speed
in the nothing, no
             nothing, no
                          nothing but speed

Flower Dream
    by Zenyatta

One night in the darkening
comfort of my stall, I dreamed

I was human—fragile—almost weightless
limber as a snake with those awful obedient

snakes sprouting out of my limbs. I was
almost a GOD, with great power

to instigate pleasure
& pain

I dreamed I was Mike himself
clinging to my own back. As one being

we circled the track
like the moon does the earth

—like the Glorious Sun—

& then we were bathed in pure sunshine
so bright we were riddled with light

until we became Light, Mike & I,
Sunshine itself

Flowers were falling from the sky
Flowers were everywhere

Beautiful, Sweet & Delicious

Breeders Choice 2010
by Joanna

("Zenyatta ran her heart out but had to settle for second")

I watch it on YouTube
I watch it again & again
I watch & keep hoping

for something to change, but nothing does—ever—
It's the same every time

At the start she's dead
last. That's expected.
She's always *dead last*

& this time she's way back
—a football field back—dirt
bashing her face

but when the time comes
she does it again

Goes into high gear
        weaving through horses
like a jet through the clouds

It's a miracle every damn time

Like an arrow she flies
        She's way faster than Blame
              & they're head to head now—
                      & she's headed for home
Except that it's over.
It's *his* name they call
Every damn time it's the same.

My Good Name*
by Zenyatta

"You better get a good name for this one," somebody said. "Because either this one is very, very fast or else we've got a farm full of very slow horses."
Bill Christine Horserace Insider 1/18/11.

I didn't even have a name
when they got me. I don't think they even give us names
before they're sure they want to keep us.

Maybe not until they race us.
We're things, you know. And I guess I had ringworm.

But Jerry knows the importance of names.
He's a rock & roll man, co-founder of A&M

records: I mean Jerry—you might say—created
The Carpenters, The Police, Janet Jackson...

I bet you don't know this about Jerry, but he's in
the Rock & Roll Hall of Fame.

So when he got word of how special I was
he came up with a powerful phrase from a powerful language
name of a powerful album: *Zenyatta Mondatta*
(That's Sanskrit for Top of the World)

& he called me Zenyatta (*on Top*)
& now he's more famous for my greatness
than he is for all of the music he ever made famous.

---

* Here Zenyatta may be mistaken. It may have been Ann who came up with the name (by Joanna)

There are jockeys & There are Jockeys!
by Joanna

& Mike Smith is more than just some little guy in tights & a helmet who rides fast horses. As he kneels at her shoulders in his shimmering greens an aura surrounds them & when she wins & wins & wins yet another & another & still another race, he flings up his arms straight out to heaven as if he were scattering blossoms of holiness over the earth, on his bright childlike face a smile so beautific he must surely be a saint. Then when she loses (which happens just that once & that the very last moment of her very last race) he folds—sobbing—into her mane: A holy being betrayed by all the powers of holiness. It was my fault he says as any saint surely would say. It was me. I wasn't pure enough.

Ruffian
by Zenyatta

Part 1

Have you heard of my hero
the great race mare Ruffian?
Darling of the 70's

                3 times Eclipse Horse of the Year

Superior they called her (strong women of the 70's)
Some girls are faster than boys, said their buttons

& then in the midst of winning at Belmont
her right foreleg   snapped.   like a toothpick

but she wouldn't stop running
Her jockey was pulling
        & pulling in vain
                on the reins

but she wouldn't stop running
& bits of her bones flew
        out onto
                the
                      track

Only then—when her hoof broke off

did she sink to the ground

& much money was lost on that race

Part II
Five veterinarians struggled to save her
but she kicked off their plasters
again & again broke
................................free of their shackles
& nothing
................not money nor prayer

could keep that mare down
long enough
to save her life

Zenyatta Retired & I have my Doubts
by Joanna

When once a great athlete
adored by the Humans

what does it mean
to be put out to pasture?

3/4 of your life left to live
(if they let you)

Checkerboard living
—no reason to run—nowhere

to run to—not even a track
to bring you full circle

again & again
or the roar of the crowds

What are you living for now, Zenyatta?
The next pat on the nose?

The next carrot?

Of course in your future:
The GREAT STUD BERNARDINI

but will you be fertile?
& if so, a good mother?

Do you love children, Zenyatta?

Zenyatta,
do you still dance?

My Own Silver Stable
    by Zenyatta

I have my own silver stable that lifts me up high into the sky
& Mario with me or sometimes it's John & everything made

just right just to please me wide open spaces & shimmering water &
pats on the nose & all around me delicious mounds & mounds

of the sweetest aloe flavored oats
& the fluffiest hay like

my pretty Ann's hair that you ever could dream of
& carrots & apples my hooves feel so light as we lift up and float

that I think I've got wings on my shoulders
& soft in my ears a deep steady hum like the breathing

& heartbeat a foal might be hearing inside the womb
they tell me in good time

if I'm good & if goddess pleases
I might be a mother

Because My Plane Was Late
    by Zenyatta

I arrived in Kentucky way after dark
to a huge peaceful crowd

waiting for me at the Keeneland racetrack

where I was paraded around
one last time by my dear humble Mario

not expected to run nor was I
to be sold but rather to be welcomed

as a hero, the star that I am, photographed
praised & adored

for my speed, beauty & goodness

& their expectations of my excellent progeny
Proudly I danced for their pleasure

It felt like a dream

Even my Jerry & Ann were there too
in the very front row of the bleachers

(they reached out to pet me as I passed by)

& then came my Mike running out onto the track
on his tiny human legs

that so often had clung to my back
as we raced on to glory

his tiny powerful godlike self

almost hidden under dark hat & coat nonetheless
still my Mike whom I love

He reached high to hug me,
pressing his face to my neck

It's Sad to See the Horses out to Pasture
by Joanna

Even you, Zenyatta, fattening in a flat, fenced in field. I know you miss the crowds. People visit now & then but it's not like it was. They call you queen & rub your nose, but already their eyes are elsewhere, looking to the future of your womb.

I wish you were out in the wild
Zenyatta. I wish you had
miles & miles of wild terrain

to run in. Even packs of wolves
to run from—
a reason to stay fast!

I wish you didn't just stand there
munching grass like any old retired mare,
dreaming of the next carrot, the next scratch on the ear

When last, Zenyatta, did you dance?

I picture a magnificent brindled stallion at the head of your herd— unlike you—never gentled. Never bought nor sold. And every way your equal. Huge, strong, smart and very, very fast & you his favorite, of course. The foals you bear together year by year so wild & free they never have to bear a human on their backs, or long for human praise & company.

Nightmare
by Zenyatta

In the dream
I was last out the gate
as usual, but somehow it didn't feel
usual. It felt sad. I was drowning in mud
& the track kept getting

l o n g e r &

        l o n g e r

                the crowd all around
booing & throwing things at me
                my legs began shrinking
beneath me
mud splashing my face so hard I was blinded

& then my right foreleg snapped off
at the ankle & then my left foreleg snapped off

at the knee I was trying to run on my tiny hind legs
awkward & slow as a human

& even those last little legs failed me completely

melting like candles held over flame
until I was left like a worm in the mud

A horse without legs
cannot run

Lane's End Farm Teaser*
    by Zenyatta

*At a breeding farm, the teaser's job is to get the ladies "interested" so they'll be ready for breeding.

I like how we hang out
—nothing to do—just hang out
me and my new

lady friends

& nobody ties us up makes us run
makes us go makes us stop

We do what we want
just so we stay inside the fence

Sometimes we race around & around
in the snow
(Of course I'm the leader)

Sometimes we bask in the sun
just plain lazy

Sometimes we kick up our hooves & play
like we haven't done since we were babies

& mornings
this real sexy stallion
(they call him Capone)

comes by my stall
& I like him. I mean I *really* like him
I like how he smells

* "She is in her stall, but we let her get nose to nose (with Capone)," Charles Campbell, the broodmare manager, said. "She's really interested in him, and that's not always the case with successful race-mares, especially ones as big and imposing as (she is)." Joe Drape, New York times News Service

Zenyatta's on Top of the World
by Joanna

Yes, yes, so she's happy
    I saw it on youtube
        what can i say?
            She's leaping & spinning
          all four feet off the ground
      Look how she nuzzles
  the newest spring grass
just coming up
  under the snow
    sun shines on her
shining black coat
  eyes shine like black coals
          she's chomping on carrots
    bundles at once
      getting her nose rubbed
        getting her chin rubbed
getting her favorite song
    sung into her ear
      getting a pat on the shoulder
        getting a pat on the rear
    look how she's prancing
    around & around
her lincoln log paddock
    tail flies like a pirate's black flag
          My god! she's even dancing

Trainer John Visits Lane's End
    by Zenyatta

Our mouth our most sensitive organ
They know this & with this they control us:

the harsh metal bit, the cold chain,
the twitch* gripping the lip, this
the most awful, causing such
an exquisite pain
that we are hypnotized
into stillness

& of course, my beloved John
knows well, this our weakness, so when he arrives
for a visit, he begins by stroking my cheeks
then my nose & then slips his
dear hand into my mouth, rubbing my gums
my so sensitive bars,
all around the teeth, the rough roof
of my mouth, the moist inner cheeks

& my strong muscled tongue, no longer lonely,
tastes his sweet hand with such joy
& such intimate knowledge

Of course I know horses, he says
to the camera. I love them.
I go into the barn & I sleep with them.

* *The horse twitch is attached to the soft, sensitive upper lip. As a result of the intense pain the twitch initially creates, the brain releases a surge of endorphins that act as natural pain killers and puts your horse in a euphoric state. Many also believe the distraction alone will keep your horse adequately occupied and that in itself will inspire him to stand quietly while you accomplish your task. (Wiki Geek)*

Sheikh Mohammed bin Khalifa bin Saeed Al Maktoum
by Zenyatta

in case you may be interested is the first cousin to

Sheikh Mohammed bin Rashid al Maktoum
(the current ruler of Dubai
& himself
a published poet
with his own facebook page)

the head of the Dubai Land Department
the land registrar of the Emirate of Dubai

& the noted owner of thoroughbred horses
including (& here come italics!)

H E to whom I am destined
to lose my virginity

the Great
B E R N A R D I N I

The Breeding Barn is dark & absolutely sterile
by Zenyatta

It went well. They say
I behaved "very professionally."

They say they are proud
pat my rump, rub my nose, my sore lip...

As for him:
It took "only one jump" ... was

"a perfect cover."

That is the language they use about us
making more of ourselves for their use

They choose us each for each.
Exchange $$$

& bring us together, tethered,
chained, twitched & scrubbed.

The twitch on my lip is
to make me. stand still

It feels almost good. Is
an odd sort of pain.

He enters in chains. Mounts on command.
Another odd pain. This time in my groin.

I do behave well. I trust them completely.
Their odd behavior is all I have known all of my life.

Then we are both scrubbed clean in our sexes
& led back to our separate vans, as ever, in chains

To My Unborn Foal
by Zenyatta

Okay so I'm Lucky
I was born blessed with speed, grace
& beauty. A desire to please.

And your father, a winner.
The best possible breeding...

Still you, my own foal, could be less
than a runner: Suppose I give birth
to a dreamer, a sleeper, a poet of horses?
What then?

In this harsh human game
we are born for
I know well how it is for the losers
If we fail on the track
we are not worth our feed.

We are sold & not always sold well.
Some of us put to hard work , some mistreated
some of us ruthlessly slaughtered
our flesh gone to feed
the descendants of wolves

Oh my sweet foal that they put in my
belly, your strong hoofless feet
beating stronger each day
at the walls of my womb

your pure equine soul
growing moment by moment
ever more perfectly
into yourself

Forgive me my weakness.
I can promise you nothing.

Zenyatta no longer "in Foal"
by Joanna

It's April Fools Day.
Zenyatta is seven today
& just the other morning
her unborn baby died.

I hadn't been checking
the last few days
so it came by surprise,

the "condolence comment"
on her website. I'm an optimist
when it comes to pregnancy.
I hadn't expected it.

& then I went out
        teaching yoga
        came home to a friend with a story
        had a round table lunch with some
        ladies, vacuumed my car
        took off my shoes
        washed yesterday's dishes
        petted my dog

but underneath my bare
feet, the floor was cold & gritty

No big deal.
It happens all the time—
especially to "maiden mares."

These Are the Races I Won
by Zenyatta

     —Breeders' Cup Ladies Classic
     —Breeders' Cup Classic
     —El Encino Stakes

     —Apple Blossom Handicap (twice)
     —Milady Handicap (twice)

     —Vanity Handicap (three times)
     —Clement L. Hirsch (three times)
     —Lady's Secret Stakes (three times)

     —Santa Margarita Handicap
     & then, Santa Margarita Handicap

These are awards I received:

     —Champion Older Female. (Three times)
     —2010 Eclipse Horse of the Year
     & THE FIRST EVER People's Choice
         Secretariat Award (2011)

These are some accolades given to me:

     —I'm the only non-human in Oprah's 2010 "O Power" List
     —I was featured in W magazine
     —MY STALL 55 IS KEPT AS A SHRINE

On October 31, 2010 over 10 million viewers
tuned in for my sake to CBS "60 Minutes."

On November 6, 2010 at least 10 billion tears
were shed for my sake

—Joanna's amongst them
    & more tears in April.

* *More Accolades (by Joanna) On September 29, 2012, a life size statue of Zenyatta was unveiled at Santa Anita Park and the race formerly known as the "Ladies Secret" was renamed "Zenyatta Stakes" in her honor. In 2016 she was inducted into the National Museum of Racing and Hall of Fame.*

Afterword, May 1, 2011
by Joanna

And so, it's already Mayday. Zenyatta is pregnant again & ever more accolades coming her way. 80,000 friends on her facebook page. Fans young and old buying their made-to-scale Breyer's Zenyattas & filming them for YouTube postings. A Texan named Dawn has just won a bronze of Zenyatta. Zenyatta's barn 55 stall, walls lined with her photos, is kept as a shrine in her honor & the *Professional Business Women of California* are including Zenyatta as the only non-human in their 2011 Annual Conference. 60 minutes is doing a follow-up program about her & all over Kentucky the tulips are in full bloom.

Postscript, August 19, 2021
by Joanna

Since her retirement to Lane's End in 2010, as a "Brood Mare," Zenyatta has been in foal 8 times to equine "royalty." Her first pregnancy, as well as her most recent pregnancy, ended in miscarriage. Her most promising foal, a filly, died in a paddock accident. According to Horse Network online, "Not one of her foals has won a single race."

www.ingramcontent.com/pod-product-compliance
Lightning Source LLC
Chambersburg PA
CBHW022126090426
42743CB00008B/1020